JAMES
V.
COLT

JAMES
V.
COLT

Hon. Andrew P. Rodovich

NATIONAL INSTITUTE FOR TRIAL ADVOCACY

Reprint Permission
National Institute for Trial Advocacy
361 Centennial Parkway, Suite 220
Louisville, Colorado 80027
Phone: (800) 225-6482
www.nita.org

ISBN: 978-1-55681-996-4

FBA0996

10 09 08 07   10 9 8 7 6 5 4 3 2 1

Printed in the United States of America

TABLE OF CONTENTS

Additional NITA case files and teaching notes by United States Magistrate Judge Andrew P. Rodovich, include:

Cosmopolitan Life Insurance Company v. Jordan	1-55681-936-6
State v. Jordan	1-55681-934-X
State v. Matthews	1-55681-902-1
State v. Patterson	1-55681-903-X
Strange v. Wrigley	1-55681-901-3
Taylor v. Pinnacle Packing Products, Inc.	1-55681-925-0
Ted Jarvis v. Columbia Breweries, Inc.	1-55681-968-4

INTRODUCTION

The plaintiff, Bart James, was convicted of distributing cocaine based on an investigation conducted by the defendant, Nita City police officer John Colt. After James' release from prison on parole, the parties had a conversation when they met in the criminal courts building while the plaintiff was on his way to meet with his parole officer. The plaintiff alleges that the defendant harassed him and threatened to return him to prison, and the defendant contends that he was investigating continued criminal conduct by the plaintiff.

On October 3, 2006, the plaintiff and defendant got into an altercation while the defendant was attempting to arrest the plaintiff, and the plaintiff was shot. The plaintiff alleges that the defendant violated his constitutional rights by using excessive force during the arrest.

The plaintiff, Bart James, and the defendant, John Colt, will testify at trial. Each party may call three additional witnesses from the following list:

Mike Bailey

Margaret Brock

Lee Butler

Robert Carpenter

Kim Nomad

Chris Panther

Trace Richards

Pat Slater

Joe Sweeny

Unless different deadlines are set by the course instructor, the plaintiff shall identify the witnesses he intends to call ten days prior to trial, and the defendant shall identify the witnesses he intends to call seven days prior to trial. A party is not required to call three witnesses, but a party must call any witness identified prior to trial.

© NATIONAL INSTITUTE FOR TRIAL ADVOCACY

CIRCUIT COURT OF DARROW COUNTY

STATE OF NITA

BART JAMES,   )
)

    Plaintiff   )
)

   v.   )
) CAUSE No. 2006 CR 111

JOHN COLT,   )
)

    Defendant   )

Complaint

Comes now the plaintiff, Bart James, and for cause of action against the defendant, John Colt, alleges and says:

1. Jurisdiction is based upon 28 U.S.C. §1331 and 42 U.S.C. §1983 because the plaintiff is claiming a violation of his constitutional rights guaranteed by the Fourth Amendment.

2. On October 3, 2006, the plaintiff was driving his vehicle when he was stopped by the defendant, a Nita City police officer.

3. The traffic stop was without probable cause and in violation of the plaintiff's Fourth Amendment rights.

4. During the traffic stop, the defendant attempted to place the plaintiff under arrest.

5. The attempted arrest was without probable cause and in violation of the plaintiff's Fourth Amendment rights.

6. During the attempted arrest, the defendant used excessive force and shot the plaintiff.

7. The use of excessive force was a violation of the plaintiff's Fourth Amendment rights.

8. The plaintiff was injured by the defendant and is entitled to compensatory and punitive damages for his personal injuries and the violations of his constitutional rights.

Wherefore, the plaintiff, Bart James, demands judgment against the defendant, John Colt, and for all other appropriate relief.

James P. Anders

__Attorney for Plaintiff__

CIRCUIT COURT OF DARROW COUNTY

STATE OF NITA

BART JAMES,   )

)

      Plaintiff   )

)

   v.   )

) CAUSE No. 2006 CR 111

JOHN COLT,   )

)

      Defendant   )

Answer

Comes now the defendant, John Colt, and in answer to the plaintiff's complaint states:

1. Admit

2. Admit

3. Deny

4. Admit

5. Deny

6. Defendant admits that the plaintiff was shot during the altercation but denies the use of excessive force.

7. Deny

8. Defendant admits that the plaintiff was injured but denies that the plaintiff is entitled to recover compensatory or punitive damages.

Wherefore, the defendant, John Colt, demands judgment against the plaintiff, Bart James, and for all other appropriate relief.

Holly Gallagher

———————————————————
Attorney for Defendant

Procedural Background

On March 16, 2007, the district court granted the defendant's motion for summary judgment with respect to the unlawful traffic stop and the false arrest claims. The district court determined that the defendant had probable cause to stop and arrest the plaintiff. The district court denied the motion with respect to the excessive force claim. Therefore, the only remaining issue for trial is whether the defendant used excessive force when he shot the plaintiff while he was attempting to place him under arrest.

STIPULATIONS

The .22 caliber handgun was registered to James Wrigley and reported stolen on January 29, 2006.

The .22 caliber bullet removed from the plaintiff during surgery was fired by the .22 caliber handgun recovered at the scene.

The white powdery substance obtained during the controlled buy of September 10, 2006, was cocaine.

The Discharge Summary from Nita General Hospital is a true and accurate record of the hospital.

The Report of the Nita State Police is a true and accurate record of the department.

Deposition of Bart James

My name is Bart James, and I live in Nita City. My friend Bob Carpenter owns a house, and I rent a room from him.

On December 16, 2002, I was convicted of distributing cocaine and received a ten-year prison sentence. Under Nita law, I served only one-third of the sentence because of good behavior. ✳ However, I am on parole for the remainder of the sentence.

I was released from prison April 16, 2006, and was instructed to report to my parole officer within ten days. My parole officer is Chris Panther, and his office is in the Nita County Criminal Courts Building in downtown Nita City.

I met with Panther on April 20, 2006, and he explained the terms of my supervision. I was required to meet with him once a month, and I had to file a monthly report concerning my activities. He also explained that I could not violate any federal, state, or municipal law.

I also was required to seek employment. My brother, Jack, buys old houses and rehabs them for rental property or for sale. My brother told me I could work for him, and he wrote a letter to Panther saying I was employed full time. I only worked for my brother when I needed the money. My main source of income was the three p's: pool, poker, and the ponies. I never told Panther I was gambling because I knew he would not approve.

My driver's license was suspended before I went to prison, and Panther helped me get a valid license after I was released. A straight flush financed a ten-year-old Buick. That was the first car I owned in more than five years.

John Colt, a Nita City police officer, was the lead investigator in the narcotics case. Sometime in May 2006, I was headed for my monthly meeting with Panther when I encountered Colt in the lobby of the courthouse. Colt recognized me immediately and asked whether I had escaped from jail. I told him I was released early because of good time credits. Colt told me that he was going to keep an eye on me and that he would be sending me back to jail sooner rather than later. I told Colt I had learned my lesson and he could watch me all day long.

I told Panther about my meeting with Colt. Panther told me that I did not have anything to worry about if I complied with the terms of my supervision. He also encouraged me to be polite to Colt if I talked to him again.

About two weeks later, I was driving within the speed limit when I saw flashing lights behind me. I pulled over immediately and looked in my rearview mirror. I had been stopped by Colt who was driving an unmarked squad car.

Colt walked up to my car and asked to see my license. I produced it for him and asked why he had stopped me. He asked me when I got my license, and I told him. Colt told me that he knew that my license had been suspended and that I was lucky I had a valid license. He dropped the license in my lap and said, "I'll get you next time."

During my next meeting with Panther, I told him about the incident. Panther told me to notify him immediately if I had any other encounters with Colt and that he would talk to Colt. However, nothing unusual happened during the next three or four months.

I am aware that Colt has prepared a police report stating that Mike Bailey acted as a confidential informant and purchased cocaine from me in September 2006. On the advice of my attorney, I refuse to answer any questions concerning any contacts that I may have had with Bailey in September 2006.

On October 1, 2006, I was playing poker with my roommate, Bob Carpenter, Bill Clark, and two other guys. I won $1,000 from Clark, but he did not have that much money with him. I told Clark that I expected the money within forty-eight hours.

On October 3, I called Clark on his cell phone and asked him whether he had the money he owed me. He told me he was working on it. I told him to meet me at the Pit Stop gas station at 4:00 P.M.

I asked Bob to go to the gas station with me in case there were any problems. I was planning to shoot pool at the Sunset Bowling Alley after I collected from Clark. Bob had other plans, so we drove to the Pit Stop in separate cars.

Clark was waiting for us when we arrived at the gas station. Bob and I got out of our cars, and Clark walked over to us. Clark pulled a wad of cash from his pocket, and I used the two of them as a shield while I counted the money. It was $1,000, so I told Clark we were square.

I did not want to take that much money to the bowling alley, so I asked Bob to take it and put it in my room. As I started to leave, Clark asked whether one of us would give him a ride to the north side of town. I told Clark I was headed for the bowling alley and asked him if he wanted to try and win his money back. He said no, and Bob told Clark he would give him a ride wherever he wanted to go. I got into my car and turned west on 16th Avenue. I do not know which direction Bob headed, but I assume it was north on Main Street.

Washington Street is the first street west of Main Street, and the bowling alley is on the corner of 12th Avenue and Main Street. I turned north on Washington Street and was planning to drive the four blocks to 12th Avenue. Washington Street is residential. I had just crossed 15th Avenue when I saw flashing lights behind me. I pulled over and looked in my rearview mirror. I saw Colt driving his unmarked car, and I was furious. I had not broken any traffic laws, and I knew he was harassing me again.] 3rd encounter

I immediately got out of my car, and Colt got out of his. Colt told me to get back into my car, and I told him I was not going to let him harass me. Colt walked toward me and again told me to return to my car. I told him I would not because he had no reason to stop me.

By this time Colt was right in front of me and told me I was under arrest. I asked him why I was ① being arrested, and he said, "For more than you can imagine." Colt told me to put my hands on my car, and I refused.

I was wearing a sweatshirt, and Colt grabbed my right sleeve and tried to turn me toward the car. ② I pulled away and told Colt to keep his hands off me because he did not have any reason to arrest me. I never pushed or punched Colt at any time.

Colt grabbed me again and tried to push me against the car, but I pulled my arm away again. The ③ third time he grabbed me, I saw him pull a small handgun from the pocket of his windbreaker. Colt said, "You asked for it" and pointed the gun at me. *

I tried to grab the gun with both hands, but he shot me before I could push the gun away from me. I felt a stabbing pain in my stomach, and I knew I had been shot.

Everything that happened after that is a blur. I remember hearing sirens and voices, but I do not know exactly what happened. I do remember talking to a paramedic in the ambulance, and she told me I was not going to die.

I was taken to the emergency room at Nita General Hospital. When I sprained my ankle about ten years ago, I had to wait over an hour to see a doctor and get X-rayed. Being shot cuts down on the wait.

I was questioned by some nurses and an emergency room doctor. I remember giving them some information, but I was in a lot of pain and not totally coherent. I do remember hearing them say something about surgery.

The next thing I remember is waking up in the recovery room and seeing my brother, Jack. He told me they removed the bullet and that the surgery was successful.

Panther came to visit me in the hospital the day after the shooting. I told him what happened, but I did not tell him about collecting a gambling debt from Clark at the Pit Stop.

An investigator from the Nita State Police also came to interview me the afternoon following the shooting. I told him Colt stopped me for no reason and that he produced a gun from his jacket pocket before shooting me.

I was not aware that the officer had talked to my brother and Bob. I told the officer I had a job working for my brother, and that I was alone when I stopped at the gas station. I did not tell him about collecting the gambling debt from Clark.

I stayed in the hospital for three days. I did not have any insurance, and the medical bills are $35,000. I was not able to work for my brother for almost a month. He was paying me between $150 and $200 each week depending on how many hours I worked. All of the payments were in cash, so I do not have any records.

I have recovered fully from the shooting, but I still have a scar on my stomach from the surgery. Part of the scar is noticeable when I have my shirt off.

I am aware that the Nita State Police determined that I pulled a gun on Colt. I never had a gun that day or at any time since I was released from prison.

I also am aware that the Nita County prosecutor has declined to file charges against me based on the Mike Bailey incident and the struggle with Colt. Panther also declined to file a petition to revoke my parole, but he warned me that I would be headed back to prison if there were any further problems.

I have not seen Colt since the incident, and I do not know whether he is still stalking me. I was collecting a gambling debt from Clark and never discussed selling him cocaine. Neither Bob nor I had any narcotics with us when we met with Clark before the shooting.

The last time I saw Clark was when he got into Bob's car at the gas station. I have no idea where he is. I have asked around, and nobody seems to know what happened to him. I have been told Clark used police funds to pay his gambling debt, so he probably is trying to avoid criminal charges. In fact, a police officer came and searched my house the day after the shooting and confiscated the money Clark gave me.

I certify that the above is a true and accurate transcript of the deposition of Bart James this

_____18_____ day of _____December_____ , 2006.

D. J. Sullivan

D. J. Sullivan

Certified Court Reporter

DEPOSITION OF JOHN COLT

My name is John Colt, and I am a detective with the Nita City Police Department. For the last six years, I have been assigned to the narcotics division.

In 2002, Trace Richards and I investigated Bart James based upon information that he was selling cocaine. Several controlled buys were made, and James was convicted in December 2002. He received a ten-year sentence.

Under Nita law, an inmate gets good time credits while in prison and can be released after serving one-third of his sentence. James was released from prison in April 2006.

James was on parole for the balance of his sentence and was assigned to Chris Panther for supervision. Panther's office is on the first floor of the Nita County Criminal Courts Building. In May 2006, I saw James in the lobby of the building when he was on his way to meet with Panther.

I was not aware that James had been released from prison and was surprised to see him. I walked up to James and asked him whether he had escaped from prison. He obviously was not happy to see me and said that he had been released in April because he had no problems in prison. I told James that I would be watching him, and if he stepped out of line I would be sending him back to prison. James told me that he had learned his lesson and that I would be wasting my time watching him.

As a narcotics officer, I frequently have informants who provide me with information. After I saw James, I asked one or two of them to let me know if they got any information on James. I also told Richards that James was out of prison, and he said he would see whether he could get any information on him.

Before he went to prison, James had a suspended driver's license. Either he would walk to a buy site or get a ride from someone. A few weeks after I saw James in the courthouse, I saw him driving a car. I was surprised because I did not believe that he had a license.

I was in an unmarked car and activated my lights when I saw James driving. James pulled over immediately, and I walked up to his car. I could tell that he was irritated, and he asked me why I had stopped him. I told James I believed that he was driving without a valid license.

James produced a valid driver's license, and I did not issue him any traffic citations. I did tell James he was lucky that he had a license and that I would continue watching him. I saw Richards later that day and told him about the traffic stop and that James had a valid license.

In early 2006, I arrested Bill Clark on narcotics charges. He agreed to cooperate, and I notified the prosecutor's office of his cooperation. Clark was charged with distributing cocaine and released on bond. He remained on bond until a warrant was issued for his arrest in October 2006.

In addition to providing information about narcotics trafficking, Clark told me that he had purchased a stolen laptop that was taken during a string of burglaries in the Walden Gardens subdivision of Nita City. I was aware of the burglaries and that Richards was in charge of the investigation.

I arranged a meeting with Richards, and Clark agreed to assist him in the burglary investigation. I was not involved in the investigation, but I am aware that a search warrant was obtained and stolen property was recovered based on information provided by Clark.

The handgun that James had on October 3, 2006, was reported stolen by James Wrigley of Walden Gardens. I was not aware that Wrigley's gun was stolen when his house was burglarized. Richards never told me what was recovered as part of his investigation. Richards did not say anything to me about the stolen gun and did not give it to me before October 3, 2006. The first time I saw that gun was when James tried to pull it on me just before he was shot.

On August 21, 2006, Richards arrested Mike Bailey for a narcotics violation. Bailey wanted to cooperate and told Richards that he had purchased cocaine from James. Richards told me about Bailey, and I agreed to assist him in the investigation of James.

Bailey said James waited a few months after he was released from prison before he started selling cocaine again. James told Bailey that I was watching him and that he was reluctant to sell cocaine on a regular basis.

Because Bailey was working for Richards, he handled all of the telephone calls to James. I was aware that a series of calls had been made and tape recorded by Richards. I told Richards to let me know when a controlled buy had been arranged.

On September 10, 2006, Richards told me that Bailey was meeting James at the Pit Stop to purchase two "8 balls" of cocaine. James had made deliveries at the Pit Stop during our last investigation. I agreed to conduct surveillance.

Richards and I went to Bailey's apartment around 2:30 P.M. Bailey was searched to ensure that he did not have any narcotics or money. We also installed a body wire to transmit any conversations with James.

Richards was responsible for driving Bailey to the buy site. I went to the Shopway strip mall across the street from the gas station to conduct surveillance. After the buy, I was going to pick up Bailey and take him back to his apartment.

I saw Bailey walk into the gas station and approach the pay phone. The only money he had was the buy money given to him by Richards, so he could not make any phone calls. About ten minutes later, James drove into the gas station.

James parked near a pump and walked into the gas station. He looked around as he was walking, and I knew he was conducting countersurveillance. He returned to the car and started pumping gas.

Bailey approached James, and they had a brief conversation. James then opened the left rear door of his car and sat down inside. I could not see what he was doing, but he had a folded newspaper in his hand when he got out of the car.

During the previous investigation, James always delivered the cocaine in a folded newspaper. After he got out of the car, James gave the newspaper to Bailey.

The body wire was transmitting the conversation between Bailey and James. James told Bailey that he only was delivering cocaine part-time because he knew I was watching him. James also told Bailey not to call him and that he would contact Bailey if he had any cocaine for sale.

James drove out of the gas station and headed north on Main Street. Bailey left the gas station and walked south on Main Street. I waited until James was out of sight and got back into my car.

When I caught up with Bailey, he was one block south of the gas station carrying the folded newspaper. He got into my car and unfolded it, revealing two baggies taped inside. I drove back to Bailey's apartment, and Richards was waiting there for us.

We went inside the apartment and gave Richards the newspaper. He opened it and saw the cocaine. We searched Bailey a second time and removed the body wire. Bailey did not have any extra money or any contraband.

Because James had told Bailey not to call him, we agreed that he should wait for a call from James. We told Bailey to mention another deal if he saw James and to call us immediately if he heard from James.

We were unable to arrange any other controlled buys between Bailey and James. Bailey reported a few brief conversations he had with James, but he told Bailey that he only was "working part-time."

I had been involved in other controlled buys with Clark, but none of these involved James. Clark had told me that he knew James and played pool with him occasionally.

On October 3, 2006, Clark called me shortly after 3:00 P.M. He told me that James had called him and offered to sell $1,000 worth of cocaine. Clark told me that James had given him until 4:00 P.M. to buy the cocaine or he would find another buyer.

Richards was out of the station when I received the call, so I paged him. Richards responded to my page and said he would return to the station when I told him about my conversation with Clark.

The police department has a policy that requires a confidential informant to wear a body wire unless it would pose a danger to him. The shift commander must be notified and approve any controlled buys without a wire.

As detectives, Richards and I were authorized to withdraw cash to be used as buy money. However, any controlled buy in excess of $500 required the approval of the shift commander.

On October 3, 2006, Lt. William Dennison was the shift commander.

Because Clark told me that he had agreed to buy $1,000 worth of cocaine, I looked for Dennison immediately after I paged Richards. I was told that Dennison and the chief were meeting with the mayor and the public safety commission at City Hall. Because we were pressed for time and Dennison was in an important meeting, I did not page him.

Richards returned to the station shortly before Clark arrived. I told him about the meeting, and he agreed that we should not page Dennison.

We also went to check out a body wire and found out that the new one already was being used by another unit. Richards and I could not get the other one to work. I did not have time to determine whether it was broken or just needed new batteries.

We searched Clark and determined that he did not have any contraband or additional cash. Richards left to set up surveillance across the street in front of Al's Ales. I drove Clark to the gas station and gave him the buy money. We left the police station at 3:45 P.M., and Clark left my car at 3:55 P.M.

I watched Clark walk to the gas station and wait for James to arrive. James came about ten minutes later and parked near the pay phone. Another car pulled in next to James. I later learned that this was his roommate, Bob Carpenter.

James and Carpenter walked up to Clark. I could see that they were talking, but I could not hear what they were saying. The three men stood close together for a few minutes and then separated. James walked back to his car and so did Carpenter. To my surprise, Clark said something to Carpenter and then got into Carpenter's car.

I did not see anything in James' hands as he walked to and from his car. He was wearing a gray sweatshirt, but I could not tell whether he had anything under the sweatshirt.

Clark had been a reliable informant and always had followed my instructions. I was concerned for his safety because I did not know why he got into the car with Carpenter.

I was in contact with Richards through police radio. I told Richards to follow Carpenter while I followed James.

I saw Carpenter leave the gas station and head north on Main Street. James turned west on 16th Avenue and then north on Washington Street. I caught up with James just after he crossed 15th Avenue.

I was in an unmarked car, and I activated my flashing lights. I also gave James a short burst with the siren to get his attention. He pulled over and stopped his car immediately.

Because I had been talking to Richards and did not want to lose sight of James, I did not radio for assistance before stopping James. Before I could report the stop and request backup, James got out of his car and started to walk toward me.

I did not want to be trapped in my car if a problem developed, so I got out quickly and instructed James to get back into his car. He was mad and accused me of harassing him. I again told James to return to his car. James stopped walking toward me, but he continued to yell at me to leave him alone.

I walked toward James and told him to get back into his car several times. He refused to follow my instructions and continued to accuse me of harassing him. I finally told James that I would arrest him if he did not get back into his car. His only response was, "What for?"

I told James that he was under arrest and to place his hands on his car. James told me that I had no grounds to arrest him and refused to lean against the car so I could frisk him. I also told James that I had more reasons to arrest him than he realized.

James was wearing a gray sweatshirt. When he refused to place his hands on the car, I grabbed the right sleeve of his sweatshirt and tried to turn him as I told him to place his hands on the car. James pulled away and told me to keep my hands off him. I grabbed his sleeve again and tried to turn him toward the car. James pulled away a second time and shoved me with both hands. The push caused me to take a step backward. I grabbed his sweatshirt a third time and again told him to put his hands on the car. I was carrying my service revolver, but I did not have a nightstick or any pepper spray. I did not attempt to pull my gun at any time.

James pulled his right arm away a third time. He is a few inches taller than I am, and he pulled his arm up as he pulled away. However, this time I saw him lift his sweatshirt with his left hand.

I immediately saw the wooden grips of a handgun in his waistband. I lowered my left shoulder and bumped James to prevent him from grabbing the gun with his right hand. I felt James' right arm across my back as I reached for the gun with my right hand.

I grabbed the gun and pulled it out of the waistband. As I took a step backward, James grabbed the gun first with his left hand and then with his right hand. James had both hands on the gun and was attempting to wrestle it out of my hand. When I put my left hand on the gun to prevent James from taking it, the gun discharged.

I heard James groan as he was hit, and he went limp and fell to the ground. I was stunned because I was not attempting to shoot him. James was on the ground and moving, so I knew he was not dead. I was going to return to my car and report the shooting when I heard sirens coming from several directions. I assumed that someone had heard the gunshot and called the police.

Within minutes, patrol officer Lee Butler approached from the south in a marked squad car, and Richards arrived from the north in his undercover vehicle.

I had many encounters with James before his 2002 conviction and while he was on parole. I never saw him with a gun, and he did not have a history of violence. I was surprised when he tried to pull a gun on me and then wrestle me for the gun. I still was in a state of shock when Richards walked up to me.

I told Richards that James tried to pull a gun on me. Richards asked me whether I was injured, and I told him I needed some time to regain my composure. Richards took the handgun and placed it on top of the car.

I walked with Richards to my car. The ambulance arrived as I was getting into my car to sit down. Kim Nomad was the paramedic in the ambulance, and she walked up to me as her partner hurried to check James. Nomad asked me whether I had been injured, and I told her I would be all right in a few minutes. Nomad then went to check on James.

I stayed at my car while the paramedics treated James. After a few minutes, the other paramedic walked past me to get the stretcher from the ambulance. He told me that James was stable and that he would survive. I was relieved to hear the news.

After James was placed in the ambulance and removed from the scene, Richards came back to my unit with the gun, a switchblade, James' wallet, and some loose change. Richards told me that Nomad had searched James and that he and Butler had searched his car, but the buy money could not be found. He also said that no narcotics or contraband were found in the car.

Because I was involved in a shooting, the Nita State Police were asked to conduct an investigation. Pat Slater was assigned to the investigation, and Richards and I were scheduled to meet with him on October 4, the next day.

Before we talked to Slater, Richards told me that he had learned the name of James' roommate. Because Clark had not followed our instructions and was a fugitive, we could not use him as a reliable source to obtain a search warrant. We asked Butler to go to James' residence and talk to Bob Carpenter, his roommate. We instructed Butler to request permission to search the house but not to threaten to get a warrant if Carpenter refused to consent.

After I gave my statement to Slater, I talked to Butler about the search. Butler said that Carpenter had consented to the search and that no guns, ammunition, narcotics, or drug paraphernalia were found. According to Butler, Carpenter claimed that Clark paid James $1,000 to satisfy a gambling debt, and Carpenter showed Butler the money that Carpenter had left in James' bedroom. Butler confiscated the money, and it was the marked money given to Clark to buy cocaine.

After the Nita State Police completed its investigation, Richards and I discussed our investigation of James with deputy prosecutor Kathy Cooper. She declined to file any charges against James stemming from the Bailey controlled buy, the transaction with Clark, or the handgun incident. She also told parole officer Chris Panther that she would not approve a petition to revoke James' parole.

I am aware that James has claimed that I pulled the .22 caliber handgun from my jacket pocket. I have two department-issued weapons, my service revolver and a shotgun, which I use on drug raids. I did not take the .22 caliber handgun with me when we were setting up the controlled buy with Clark.

I arranged for Clark to talk to Richards about the burglary investigation, but I did not assist Richards in getting the search warrant or recovering any property. I have no idea what property was reported stolen in the burglaries or what was recovered by Richards.

Cooper filed a petition to revoke Clark's bond because he became a fugitive. A warrant was issued for his arrest, and we have not been able to locate him. Cooper also declined to file theft charges against Clark for using the buy money to pay James for a gambling debt.

I certify that the above is a true and accurate transcript of the deposition of John Colt this

_____21_____ day of _____December_____ , 2006.

D. J. Sullivan

D. J. Sullivan
Certified Court Reporter

DEPOSITION OF MIKE BAILEY

My name is Mike Bailey, and I currently am confined at the Nita State Prison. I was convicted of possession of cocaine and received a six-year prison sentence. With time off for good behavior, I will be released in December 2008.

I have known Bart James for many years. We played pool at the Sunset Bowling Alley, and I bought cocaine from him before he was convicted in 2002.

I saw Bart shortly after he was released from prison, and I asked him whether he was going back into business. Bart told me that the cops were watching him and that he was playing it safe for a few months. I told Bart to let me know when he started selling again.

In July 2006, Bart asked me whether I still was interested in buying cocaine. He told me he had a new supplier and that he was starting to sell cocaine again. A few days later, I bought an eighth of an ounce of cocaine, known as an "8 ball," from Bart. I made other purchases from him over the next several weeks.

On August 21, 2006, I was arrested for dealing cocaine. One of my customers had been a confidential informant. I had a prior record, and I knew that I was in big trouble.

Trace Richards was the investigating officer on my case. Richards and John Colt had been involved in the case that sent Bart to prison in 2002. I immediately told Richards that I wanted to cooperate and that I could make a purchase from Bart.

On September 6, 2006, I called Bart on his cell phone. Richards monitored the call, and it was tape recorded. I told Bart I needed two "8 balls." Bart told me he was only working part-time and that he might have some cocaine in a few days.

I called Bart again on September 9, 2006. Richards again monitored the call, and it was tape recorded. Bart told me he would have some cocaine the next day and that I could have two "8 balls" for $350. Bart told me to call him around 10:00 A.M.

I called Bart on September 10, 2006, after 10:00 A.M. The call was tape recorded by Richards. We agreed to meet at the Pit Stop gas station at 3:00 P.M.

Richards and Colt came to my apartment at 2:30 P.M. They searched me and determined that I did not have any money or narcotics on my person. They also installed a body wire to transmit my conversations with Bart. Richards drove me to within one block of the gas station and gave me $350 in cash. We also checked to see whether the body wire was working, and it was.

I agreed to walk south on Main Street after the buy. Colt was conducting surveillance from the Shopway strip mall across the street, and he was going to pick me up after Bart left the area.

I got to the gas station a few minutes before 3:00 P.M. I pretended to use the pay phone at the southeast corner of the gas station. I did not have anything in my pockets except the cash given to me by the police, so I could not call anyone.

Bart came about ten minutes later. He parked his car near a pump and went inside to pay for the gas. He was looking around as he walked to and from the building. I knew that he was conducting countersurveillance.

As Bart started to pump the gas, I walked up to him. We exchanged greetings, and I gave him the money. Bart opened the left rear door of his car and sat down to count the money. He then picked up a folded newspaper on the floor of the car and gave it to me. I unfolded the paper part way and noticed two baggies taped inside. Bart always delivered the cocaine in a folded newspaper.

By this time the pump had clicked off, and Bart placed the nozzle back on the pump. He told me that he was working part-time because Colt had threatened him, and Bart felt like he was being watched. Bart told me not to call him but he would call me the next time he had cocaine to sell.

Bart got back into his car and drove north on Main Street. I assumed that he was heading to the bowling alley to play pool. I left the gas station and started walking south on Main Street.

After I had walked for a few minutes, Colt picked me up and drove me back to my apartment. Richards was waiting for us, and we went inside. I gave them the newspaper, and they opened it and removed the cocaine. They searched me a second time to verify that I did not have any other contraband or any of the drug money.

I removed the body wire and gave it to Colt. Because Bart had told me not to call him, we agreed to wait until I heard from Bart again. I told them I would remind Bart that I was interested in buying more cocaine if I saw him at the bowling alley.

I saw Bart at the bowling alley about a week later. I asked him when he expected another delivery, and he said he did not know. He mentioned that he had won some money at the racetrack and would be selling cocaine only when he needed some money quickly. He laughed and said that selling cocaine was easier than working for his brother.

I did not see Bart before he was shot, and I was not involved with any more controlled buys before the shooting.

I have never seen Bart with a gun. Bart had on a baggy shirt when I made the buy from him on September 10. I cannot say for sure, but I do not believe that he had a gun under his shirt. I never got in his car that day, but I did not see a gun when the left rear door was open.

I originally was charged with possession of cocaine with intent to deliver. Richards spoke to the prosecutor on my behalf, and the charge was reduced to simple possession of cocaine. Under the original charge, I faced a maximum of twenty years in prison. I signed a plea agreement that gave me six years in prison. I also agreed to testify truthfully in any proceedings against Bart.

I certify that the above is a true and accurate transcript of the deposition of Mike Bailey this

_____19_____ day of _____December_____ , 2006.

D. J. Sullivan

_____

D. J. Sullivan

Certified Court Reporter

DEPOSITION OF MARGARET BROCK

My name is Margaret Brock, and I live at 1436 Washington Street in Nita City. My husband is dead, and I live alone.

Every afternoon I watch Jeopardy from 3:30 to 4:00 P.M. Jeopardy had just ended, and I had a few things I wanted to do before dinner. Although I am not sure of the exact time, I believe it was about 4:10 P.M. when I saw flashing lights from my bedroom window.

The front of my house faces east, and I saw an unmarked police car, with its lights flashing, parked across the street from my house, heading north. Another car was parked about 20 feet in front of the squad car.

The drivers had gotten out of the cars and were walking toward each other. The police officer was wearing a dark windbreaker and was not in uniform. The other man was wearing a gray sweatshirt.

I could not hear what they were saying, but I could tell that they were having a heated discussion as the officer approached the other man. The officer repeatedly gestured toward the car, and it seemed like the officer was ordering him to get back in the car. Everything happened very fast, so I cannot say how long I was watching.

The officer then grabbed the man by his right arm and tried to push him against the car. The man pulled back, and the officer grabbed his right arm a second time.

I immediately picked up the phone next to my bed and called 911. An operator answered after the first ring. I gave my name and address and started to say that a police officer was involved in an altercation in front of my house and needed assistance.

Before I finished my report, I heard a shot. I yelled, "Someone's been shot!" and looked out my window. I saw the officer holding a gun and the man lying on the ground.

I told the operator that the officer had shot the man. I could hear the operator saying something using police codes. I assumed that she had radioed for assistance. In less than a minute, I heard sirens coming from all directions. I walked to my living room to look out of my picture window. I saw the officer just standing there holding the gun. It did not appear as if he had moved since I last saw him.

I could see that the man on the ground was moving, so I knew he was not dead. Within minutes of my call, two other police cars arrived at the scene. One came from the north, and the other came from the south.

The sirens continued, and a minute or two later the ambulance arrived. It parked directly in front of my house, and I could not see what they were doing. Several minutes later, I saw them place the man in the rear of the ambulance.

After the ambulance left, a police officer in uniform came to my front door. He thanked me for calling 911 and told me that an investigator from the Nita State Police would be contacting me within a few hours. He said the state police investigated all police shootings.

Around 6:30 P.M., someone from the Nita State Police came to my front door. I told him exactly what I had seen. I did not see a gun before I dialed 911 and was startled when I heard the gunshot. I do not know who pulled the gun or where it came from.

I certify that the above is a true and accurate transcript of the deposition of Margaret Brock this

_____19_____ day of _____December_____ , 2006.

D. J. Sullivan
Certified Court Reporter

DEPOSITION OF LEE BUTLER

My name is Lee Butler, and I am a patrol officer with the Nita City Police Department. On October 3, 2006, I was working the afternoon shift in the downtown section of Nita City. I was in uniform and driving a marked squad car.

Around 4:20 P.M. I received a dispatch that a police officer was involved in a shooting in the 1400 block of Washington Street. I activated my lights and siren and went directly to the scene. I was on the east side of Main Street when I received the call, and it took me two or three minutes to get to the scene.

I approached the two parked vehicles from the south. Detective Trace Richards was in an unmarked car, and he arrived from the north as I was coming to a stop. Richards got out of his vehicle and approached Detective John Colt.

As I exited my unit, I saw Bart James lying in the street and Colt holding a handgun. I reported the situation back to headquarters and confirmed that an ambulance had been sent. As it turned out, the sirens I was hearing came from the ambulance and not another squad car.

Colt and Richards had a brief discussion, and I saw Colt place the gun on top of James' car. Richards then escorted Colt back to his squad car. By this time I had completed my update and went to check on Colt. He was upset but told me he had not been shot.

When the ambulance arrived, I walked over to check James with the paramedic. I also was concerned because a crowd was gathering, and I made sure they stayed away from the vehicles and any potential evidence.

Paramedic Kim Nomad had stopped to check Colt and then walked over to assist the paramedic treating James. Nomad told me that James would survive and that he would be taken to the hospital shortly.

As I was talking to Nomad, Richards approached and asked Nomad to empty the pockets of James. I saw a wallet, some loose change, and a switchblade taken from James. Nomad gave these items to Richards. I did not see how much money was in the wallet, but I know that Nomad did not find a large amount of cash.

I watched Richards as he searched James' car. Richards told me that he and Colt had set up a controlled buy and that he was looking for the buy money and any drug paraphernalia.

Richards did not find any money or contraband. I helped Richards look for secret compartments in the car, but we could not find any.

The paramedics removed James from the scene, and I returned to the station to file my report. Because the shooting involved a Nita City police officer, I knew that the Nita State Police would be asked to investigate the incident.

The next day, Richards asked me to go to James' residence and ask his roommate, Robert Carpenter, for permission to search the house. Richards told me that he and Colt were not going to request a search warrant because their informant had disappeared and they no longer considered him credible. Richards told me not to press the issue if Carpenter would not grant me permission to search.

I went to Carpenter's house around 11:00 A.M. on October 4, 2006. I was in my uniform and drove a marked squad car. I identified myself when Carpenter answered the door. I told Carpenter that I did not have a warrant to search his house and requested permission to conduct a search. Carpenter said that he and James had nothing to hide and that I could search anywhere I wanted.

Carpenter escorted me to James' bedroom and pointed out $1,000 in cash lying on his bed. He told me that Clark paid James $1,000 to satisfy a gambling debt and that he had put the money in James' bedroom because James had left the gas station to play pool. I told Carpenter that the money came from police department funds, and Carpenter did not object to me seizing the money.

I thoroughly searched James' bedroom and the rest of the house, including Carpenter's bedroom. I did not find any guns, ammunition, narcotics, or drug paraphernalia. As I completed the search, Carpenter told me he never had seen James with a gun or narcotics while James lived with him.

I returned to the station and gave the $1,000 to Richards. He compared the money to his records and confirmed that it was the buy money given to Clark. I also told Richards that Carpenter was cooperative and that I did not find any incriminating evidence during the search.

I certify that the above is a true and accurate transcript of the deposition of Lee Butler this _____19_____ day of _____December_____ , 2006.

D. J. Sullivan

_____

D. J. Sullivan

Certified Court Reporter

Deposition of Robert Carpenter

My name is Robert Carpenter, and I live in Nita City. I have known Bart James since we were in high school. About five years ago I bought an old house, and Jack James, Bart's brother, helped me remodel it.

Bart was released from prison in April 2006. I had an extra bedroom in my house, and I told Bart he could rent a room from me.

In 1999, I was arrested for possession of marijuana, a misdemeanor, and pled guilty. I was fined $500 plus court costs.

Bart's brother, Jack, buys old houses to rehab. I have worked for him for short periods of time. Bart showed me a letter Jack had written saying that Bart was working full-time. Bart only worked for Jack when he was short on money.

Bart prefers to make a living as a gambler. I have played pool with him, but never for money because he is a hustler. He can string someone along and barely win a game if he thinks he can up the ante or entice the pigeon into playing more games.

Bart also is skilled at poker. We frequently have games at my house. Occasionally, Bart has a bad night, but not often.

I am aware that Bart was convicted of dealing cocaine in 2002. I never saw Bart with any narcotics or paraphernalia after he moved in with me. If I had seen any narcotics, I would have told Bart to move out. I do not need any trouble with the authorities.

I have played cards and pool with Mike Bailey many times. I never heard Bart and Mike discussing cocaine sales, and I do not know anything about a controlled buy that supposedly occurred in September 2006.

A few days before Bart was shot, we were playing cards with Bill Clark and two other guys. Bart won $1,000 from Clark. Bart told Clark he would give him forty-eight hours to get the money. The afternoon Bart was shot he told me he was meeting Clark at the Pit Stop to collect his money. Bart asked me to go with him in case there were any problems.

Bart and I drove to the Pit Stop separately. He was going to play pool at Sunset, and I had some errands I had to get done. Clark was at the gas station when we arrived. We got out of our cars, and Clark walked up to us. He gave Bart a wad of bills. Bart turned toward the car to count the money, and I stood near Bart so no one could see how much money he had.

Bart told Clark they were even and asked me to put the money in his room. Clark asked whether one of us would give him a ride to the north side of town. Bart declined and told Clark he was going to play pool at the bowling alley. He asked Clark whether he wanted a chance to win his money back, but Clark said no.

I told Clark I would give him a ride. We got in my car and headed north on Main Street. I dropped Clark off at the intersection of Main Street and Broadway, which is sixteen blocks north of the gas station. Clark got out of the car, and I have not seen him since.

Bart was wearing a gray sweatshirt when we left the house. Bart is in good shape, and the sweatshirt was a little baggy around the waist. I never have seen Bart with a gun in my house, and I do not believe he was carrying one when we left for the Pit Stop. However, I cannot say for sure.

I never go into Bart's room when he is gone. He gave me the $1,000 and asked me to put it in his room. I walked into his room and dropped the money on his bed and left. I did not see anything to suggest that he had guns or drugs in the room.

I got a call later that evening from Jack telling me that his brother had been shot. I went to the hospital to be with Jack while Bart was in surgery. I did not see Bart until late the next morning, and he was in a lot of pain.

On October 4, a police officer named Lee Butler and another officer knocked on my front door. Butler told me he did not have a warrant, but he asked whether he could search my house. I told him they could come in and look around because Bart and I had nothing to hide.

I showed them Bart's room and told them that the $1,000 he received from Clark was on his bed. They confiscated that money and went through his dresser and closet. They also searched my room and the rest of the house. The police did not find any narcotics or drug paraphernalia and did not take anything from the house except the $1,000 in cash.

Bart came home three days later. He spent a lot of time around the house for the next month or so. Bart told me that Panther gave him hell for lying about working for Jack. Five or six weeks after the shooting, Bart started working for Jack full-time. He still gambles occasionally, but he does not do it as his primary source of income anymore.

I certify that the above is a true and accurate transcript of the deposition of Robert Carpenter this _____20_____ day of _____December_____ , 2006.

D. J. Sullivan

_____

D. J. Sullivan

Certified Court Reporter

DEPOSITION OF KIM NOMAD

My name is Kim Nomad, and I am a paramedic with the Nita City Fire Department. On October 3, 2006, I was assigned to ambulance No. 3.

I have been a paramedic for nine years. I have responded to hundreds of traffic accidents and have treated people for both minor and life-threatening injuries. I also have responded to other medical emergencies such as heart attacks and strokes. Because Nita City is a large metropolitan area, I frequently get dispatched to a crime scene and treat gunshot and knife wounds.

On October 3, 2006, I was notified by police dispatch of a shooting in the 1400 block of Washington Street. I was told that an officer had been involved and that someone had been wounded. The dispatch came in at 4:19 P.M., and we arrived at the scene at 4:26 P.M.

As we approached the scene of the shooting, I saw a marked squad car with flashing lights facing north and an unmarked squad car with flashing lights heading south. There were two vehicles facing north, which were parked between the police units. I immediately noticed a man lying in the street next to the Buick that was parked near the unmarked squad car.

I have known Trace Richards and John Colt for many years. I have responded to accidents and crime scenes where they were investigating officers. As the ambulance came to a stop, I saw Colt and Richards standing next to the second parked car. I then recognized this as another unmarked squad car.

Before we got out of the ambulance, I told my partner, Dave Peters, to check on the shooting victim while I talked to Richards and Colt. I did not know which officer had been involved in the shooting or if he had been injured.

I walked up to Colt and Richards and asked what happened. Colt told me he was involved in a struggle over a handgun and that he had shot the other man. Colt seemed calm and described what happened in a normal tone of voice. I asked Colt if he had been injured, and he told me he was "fine." I then went to check on the shooting victim, and Colt and Richards remained near Colt's car for a few minutes talking.

I checked with Peters, and he told me the patient was stable. I later learned that his name was Bart James, but he was in no condition to provide me with any information. I stayed with James while Peters returned to the ambulance to get the stretcher.

James was in pain and responded to some questions when he was called by name. I tried to reassure him that he would be all right, and he seemed to respond to those comments.

Peters returned with the stretcher. Before we could load James on the stretcher, Richards asked me to remove all the belongings from James' pockets. I gave Richards a wallet, some coins, and a closed switchblade. I did not count the money in the wallet. Richards seemed irritated and asked me whether I was sure that I got everything. I told him I had emptied all of the pockets.

As we were putting James on the stretcher, Richards and patrol officer Lee Butler were searching James' car. I do not know what they were looking for or what they found.

After we put James in the back of the ambulance, Colt asked me what his condition was. I told Colt the wound was not life-threatening, and he seemed relieved. Before I climbed into the ambulance with James, I again asked Colt whether he needed any assistance. Colt repeated that he was "fine."

Peters drove the ambulance, and I rode in the back to monitor James. He was restless and in obvious pain. I told him we would be at the hospital soon.

Nita General Hospital was about a five-minute ride from the scene. We took James into the emergency room and released him to the hospital staff. James was stable but not entirely lucid when we left the emergency room.

I never asked either Colt or James how the shooting occurred. My job is to treat an injured person and let the authorities and the court determine what happened. I am not qualified to say how a shooting occurred or how a gun was positioned when it was discharged.

I certify that the above is a true and accurate transcript of the deposition of Kim Nomad this

_____20_____ day of _____December_____ , 2006.

D. J. Sullivan

_____

D. J. Sullivan

Certified Court Reporter

Deposition of Chris Panther

My name is Chris Panther, and I am employed by the Nita County Circuit Court as a probation officer. I have been a probation officer for twenty years.

My office is on the first floor in the Nita County Criminal Courts Building. After a defendant has been convicted of a crime, I prepare a pre-sentence report for the judge. This report includes the personal background of the defendant, his prior record, and any information provided by the victim of the crime.

If a defendant is placed on probation, I am responsible for his supervision during the term set by the court. A defendant who receives a jail sentence is eligible for release after serving one-third of his term if he does not get into any trouble in prison. A defendant released from prison is on parole for the balance of his sentence.

The rules for supervision are the same regardless of whether the defendant is on probation or parole. I explain the requirements to each defendant during our first meeting, and the defendant is required to sign a form acknowledging that he understands the requirements of supervision.

A defendant may not violate any federal, state, or local law while on supervision. A violation can result in the revocation of probation or parole, in addition to any penalty imposed for the new offense.

A defendant also is required to seek employment and provide me with proof of employment. Finally, a defendant must fill out a monthly report and provide me a copy by the 10th of each month.

I prepared the pre-sentence report when Bart James was convicted and sentenced in 2002. He received a ten-year sentence and was released on parole on April 16, 2006. Prison officials instructed Bart to report to me within ten days, and he reported on April 20, 2006.

© National Institute for Trial Advocacy

During the first meeting, I explained the terms of supervision to Bart, and he signed the required form. Bart told me that his brother, Jack, bought old houses to rehab and then sell or rent. Bart said his brother offered him a job cleaning and remodeling old houses.

Bart was required to meet with me once a month, and a meeting was scheduled for May 23. When Bart arrived, he was noticeably upset. He told me he had just seen John Colt, the investigating officer on his drug case, in the lobby of the building. According to Bart, Colt asked him whether he had escaped from prison and told Bart that he would be sending him back as soon as he could.

I told Bart he did not have anything to worry about if he complied with the terms of his supervision. I also encouraged him to be polite to Colt so that Colt would not have any additional incentives to watch him. Bart next came into my office on June 22, 2006. He told me that Colt had stopped his vehicle a few weeks earlier and demanded to see his driver's license. Bart said Colt was upset that Bart had a valid license and again threatened to send him back to prison. I told Bart to let me know immediately if he had any other encounters with Colt and that I would contact Colt if the problem continued. Bart never complained about Colt in any other meetings before he was shot.

In all of his monthly reports, Bart said that he was working thirty to forty hours a week for his brother. I also received a letter from his brother, Jack, stating that Bart was working steadily. Because Bart did not have a fixed place of employment, I never attempted to verify that he was working.

Bart never told me he was gambling instead of working for his brother. I did not learn of this until I reviewed the police reports following the shooting. If I had known about his gambling, I would have told Bart that he was violating the terms of his supervision. Gambling violates state law and also puts him in contact with other convicted felons. I would have monitored Bart more closely if I had known that he was gambling. If he continued to gamble, I would have petitioned the court to revoke his parole.

Bart was shot on October 3, 2006, and I was notified at home that evening. I also was told that the injuries were not life threatening and that Bart had been taken to surgery.

I went to the hospital the next day to see Bart on my way home from work. He was alert but obviously in some pain. As soon as I walked into the room, Bart said, "I told you that SOB was out to get me."

Bart told me he had stopped to get gas at the Pit Stop and then was meeting some friends at the Sunset Bowling Alley. Bart said he left the gas station by turning right on 16th Avenue and right again on Washington Street. He had gone only a few blocks when he saw flashing lights behind him.

Bart said he had not committed a traffic violation, but he pulled over immediately. When he looked in his rearview mirror and saw Colt, Bart said he "lost it."

Bart jumped out of his car to confront Colt. Bart said that Colt got out of his unmarked car and told him to get back into his car. When Bart refused, Colt approached him and again told Bart to get back into his car.

Bart claimed that he was standing next to his car the whole time and never threatened Colt or moved toward him. Colt had continued to approach Bart and told him that he was under arrest. Bart demanded to know why he was being arrested, but Colt grabbed Bart's right arm and attempted to push him against the car.

Bart admitted that he pulled his arm away from Colt but denied pushing or striking Colt in any fashion. Colt again grabbed Bart's arm, and Bart pulled away and would not lean against the car. As Colt grabbed Bart a third time, he saw Colt pull a handgun from the pocket of his windbreaker. Colt said, "You asked for it," and pointed the gun at Bart.

Bart claimed that he grabbed the gun and tried to point it away from him but it went off. He felt a sharp pain in his stomach and fell to the ground.

Bart could not remember what happened next, but he said Colt did not hit him or shoot him a second time. Bart said he was in a lot of pain and vaguely remembered being treated at the scene and being taken to the hospital.

I am aware that Bart now claims he went to the Pit Stop to collect a gambling debt from a man named Bill Clark. Bart never said anything to me about receiving $1,000 from Clark, or that he gave the money to his roommate for safekeeping.

If a Nita City police officer is involved in a shooting, it is standard practice to ask the Nita State Police to investigate the incident. On October 5, 2006, NSP detective Pat Slater contacted me as part of the investigation. I provided a statement concerning Bart's activities while on parole and what he told me at the hospital.

On October 12, 2006, I contacted Nita County deputy prosecutor Kathy Cooper. She had prosecuted Bart in 2002 and was reviewing all of the evidence concerning the investigation of Bart and the shooting.

Kathy told me no one had been able to locate Bill Clark. According to his landlord, Clark turned in the key to his apartment on October 3, 2006, and did not leave a forwarding address. The Nita State Police also have not been able to locate Clark.

Kathy also told me about a controlled buy from Mike Bailey on September 10, 2006. According to Trace Richards, Bart sold Bailey two "8 balls" of cocaine for $350. Colt was conducting surveillance during the controlled buy.

According to the NSP report, a search of Bart's car after the shooting did not uncover any narcotics, guns, or the buy money.

Kathy told me she had decided not to file any new charges against Bart and suggested that I not file a petition to revoke his parole. She felt that one controlled buy would be difficult to prove, especially with the problems between Bart and Colt.

I agreed with Kathy and did not file a petition to revoke Bart's parole. However, I warned him that I would be watching him more carefully and that a petition would be filed if he had any additional problems.

I also instructed Bart that he could not gamble or even go inside the bowling alley. I talked to Bart's brother and told him that Bart would be returning to jail if he did not work. Bart and his brother have provided me with a weekly work schedule, and I have stopped at the houses to verify that Bart has been working.

I have not had any problems with Bart since the shooting. To my knowledge, he has complied with all of the conditions of his release and does not want to return to prison.

I certify that the above is a true and accurate transcript of the deposition of Chris Panther this

_____20_____ day of _____December_____ , 2006.

D. J. Sullivan
Certified Court Reporter

DEPOSITION OF TRACE RICHARDS

My name is Trace Richards, and I am a detective with the Nita City Police Department. In 2002, my partner, John Colt, and I were the investigating officers when Bart James was convicted of distributing cocaine.

Under Nita law, someone is eligible for parole after serving one-third of his sentence. The offender then is on parole for the balance of the sentence. Parole can be revoked if the offender does not comply with the terms of his supervision or if he commits another crime.

The probation and parole officers work in the Nita County Criminal Courts Building. Colt and I are in the building regularly to meet with the prosecutor's office or to testify at trial.

In May 2006, Colt told me he had been in the criminal courts building and had seen James. Colt said he had a short conversation with James and told James that he would be watching him. I told Colt I would contact some of my confidential informants and ask them to let me know if they heard anything about James.

Before James went to prison, Colt and I knew that he had a suspended driver's license. A few weeks after Colt told me he saw James in the criminal courts building, Colt told me he had stopped James for driving without a driver's license. Colt said he was surprised that James had obtained a valid license. He added, "I thought that it was too easy."

On August 21, 2006, I arrested Mike Bailey for selling cocaine. Bailey told me he knew that I was the investigating officer on James' case and that he had purchased cocaine from James since his release from prison. Bailey said James was concerned that he was being watched and waited a few months before he started selling cocaine again.

When Bailey agreed to cooperate, I told Colt I had a confidential informant who claimed that he had purchased cocaine from James. Colt agreed to help me with the investigation.

On September 6, 2006, Bailey called James on his cell phone, and I recorded the call. Bailey asked for two "8 balls" or two baggies containing 1/8 ounce of cocaine. James said he only was working part-time and that Bailey should check with him in a few days. "Part-time" was his term for not dealing cocaine on a regular basis.

Bailey called James again on September 9, 2006, and I tape recorded the call. James said he would have cocaine the next day, and he would sell Bailey two "8 balls" for $350. James told Bailey to call back around 10:00 A.M. the next day.

Bailey called James shortly after 10:00 A.M., and I recorded the call. Bailey agreed to meet James at the Pit Stop gas station at 3:00 P.M. I notified Colt that a controlled buy had been arranged.

Colt and I went to Bailey's apartment around 2:30 P.M. We searched him and determined that he did not have any contraband or money. We also installed a body wire to record the transaction.

I drove Bailey to the vicinity of the Pit Stop and gave him $350 in cash. The money had been photocopied so the serial numbers were recorded. Bailey and I activated the body wire and tested it before he walked to the gas station.

Colt was across the street from the gas station in the Shopway strip mall. After conducting surveillance, Colt was scheduled to pick up Bailey as he walked away from the gas station.

I watched Bailey walk to the gas station and pretend to use the pay phone. Because he did not have any coins and the body wire was working, I know he did not make any phone calls.

James came after Bailey had been in the gas station for ten or fifteen minutes. He parked near a pump and went inside to pay for the gas. I saw James looking around as he walked to and from his car. I knew he was conducting countersurveillance.

I saw Bailey approach James as he was pumping gas. After a brief conversation, James opened the left rear door of his car and sat down inside. I could not see him, but I assumed he was counting the money.

When James got out of the car, he was holding a folded newspaper.

During the controlled buys leading up to his conviction, James always delivered the cocaine in a folded newspaper. James gave the newspaper to Bailey.

James completed the gas transaction as he talked to Bailey. I heard James tell Bailey that he was only working part-time because Colt had threatened him. James also told Bailey not to call him and that he would call Bailey when he had any cocaine to distribute.

James got into his car and drove out of the gas station. Bailey started walking south on Main Street as we had agreed. I waited a few minutes to be sure that James had left the area and returned to Bailey's apartment.

Colt picked up Bailey, and they arrived at the apartment a few minutes after I got there. We went inside and examined the newspaper. It had two baggies of a white powdery substance taped inside. Colt and I searched Bailey a second time, and he did not have any money or contraband. We also removed the body wire.

We told Bailey not to call James based on his instructions but to ask about another buy if he saw him someplace. We also told Bailey to call us if James contacted him about another sale.

Colt had arrested Bill Clark on a narcotics charge early in 2006. Clark made some controlled buys for Colt, but I was not involved in them. Clark also provided Colt with some information concerning a burglary ring operating in the Walden Gardens subdivision of Nita City. Because I was handling that investigation, Colt arranged for me to meet with Clark.

In January and February 2006, seven homes were burglarized in the subdivision. The burglars mainly took electronic items such as computers, television sets, and microwave ovens. Some homeowners reported that cash and jewelry were stolen, and two reported stolen handguns.

Clark told me that Steve Bradley lived in Walden Gardens and had stolen electronic equipment in his basement. Clark also provided me with a laptop that he bought from Bradley on April 3, 2006. A check of the burglary reports revealed that the computer was the property of James and Kathy Wrigley. The Wrigleys also reported that a .22 caliber handgun had been stolen.

Based on the information provided by Clark, I obtained a search warrant for Bradley's house. The warrant was executed on April 6, 2006. A large number of electronic items were recovered, but no cash, jewelry, or handguns were found. Bradley also gave a statement admitting to the burglaries, and formal charges were filed against him.

Other than the burglary investigation, I did not have any more dealings with Clark before October 3, 2006. Everything he had told me during the burglary investigation proved accurate, and I believed that he was a reliable, confidential informant. Colt never complained to me about having any problems with Clark.

On October 3, I received a page from Colt and called him. Colt told me that Clark had received a call from James and had agreed to buy cocaine at 4:00 P.M. This left us less than an hour to make the arrangements, so I returned to the station immediately. Clark arrived at the station a short time later.

The police department has two policies that created a problem for Colt and me. A confidential informant must wear a body wire for any controlled buy unless there is a reason to believe that a wire would endanger the confidential informant. Also, an officer needs the approval of the shift commander before using more than $500 to purchase narcotics.

Lt. William Dennison was the shift commander that afternoon. When Colt and I looked for him, we were told that he and the chief were meeting with the mayor and the public safety commission. We decided not to page Dennison because Clark had been reliable in the past and we were short on time.

The department has two body wires. Another unit had checked out the newer one, and we could not get the older one to operate. I do not know whether it was broken or just needed new batteries, but we did not have time to fiddle with it. Colt and I agreed to send Clark to make the buy without the wire and without the approval of Dennison.

We obtained $1,000 in cash and photocopied the bills in case an arrest was made later. We searched Clark and determined that he did not have any money or contraband. We gave him the $1,000 and left the station around 3:45 P.M.

Colt drove Clark to the buy site, and I conducted surveillance from Al's Ales, a liquor store across the street from the gas station. I saw Clark walk into the gas station, and James arrived about ten minutes later.

James was in his car, and another car parked next to James. I later learned that the second man was Bob Carpenter, James' roommate. Both men walked up to Clark, and they stood close together. I could not see what was happening, and the three men separated after a few minutes.

James was wearing a gray sweatshirt. I did not see anything in his hands when he walked to meet with Clark or when he returned to his car. From that distance, I could not tell whether he had a gun or anything else under his sweatshirt.

The three of them were talking as James and Carpenter walked back to their cars. I was surprised when I saw Clark get into Carpenter's car with him. Without the benefit of a body wire, I had no idea what was said and was concerned for the safety of Clark.

Colt and I had maintained contact through police radio. Obviously Colt had no idea why Clark was leaving with Carpenter. We agreed that Colt would follow James and that I would follow Carpenter.

I was conducting surveillance outside of my vehicle. Carpenter turned out of the gas station and headed north on Main Street. Traffic was heavy, and by the time I got back into my car and on Main Street, I had lost sight of Carpenter. I tried to maneuver through traffic, but I could not catch up with him.

I had driven about one mile when I received a dispatch about a shooting in the 1400 block of Washington Street. I activated my lights and siren and turned left off Main Street and left again on Washington Street. As I was approaching the scene of the shooting, I saw patrol officer Lee Butler arriving from the south.

I got out of my car and hurried over to Colt. He was holding a handgun, and James was lying on the ground. James was moving, so I knew that he was not dead.

Colt was very upset, and his hands were shaking. Before I could say anything, Colt said, "He tried to pull a gun on me." I asked Colt if he was injured and he said "no."

Colt offered me the gun, and I told him to put it on top of the car. I took Colt by the arm and escorted him back to his car. As Colt was getting into his car, the ambulance arrived. One paramedic went to check James, and paramedic Kim Nomad walked up to Colt.

Nomad asked Colt if he was injured, and he said he only was shaken up. Colt said all he needed was time to compose himself. Nomad then went to assist James.

After I stayed with Colt for a few minutes, I went to check on the condition of James. Nomad told me that James was stable and that they would be removing him from the scene shortly. I asked Nomad to remove all of James' personal belongings from his pockets and watched as some coins, a wallet, and a switchblade were recovered. The switchblade measured 8 inches when opened.

I also searched the car and did not find any additional money, cocaine, or drug paraphernalia. The wallet contained $200 but not any of the buy money. I also checked to see whether there were any hidden compartments in the car and could not find any.

I removed the gun from the roof of the car and was careful not to disturb any fingerprints that may have been on the weapon. I took it to the police station and later gave it to Detective Pat Slater of the Nita State Police.

The next day, I learned that Carpenter was James' roommate. Because Clark had fled the scene and could not be located, I could not represent to a judge that he was a reliable informant. Colt and I agreed that we should not request a warrant to search the residence.

Colt and I were scheduled to be interviewed by Slater, so we asked Butler to go to Carpenter's residence. We told him to request permission to search the house and to leave if permission was denied.

Later that day, Butler came back and reported that Carpenter had consented to a search of the entire house. No drugs or drug paraphernalia were found, but Butler seized $1,000 from James' bedroom. Carpenter said the $1,000 was the money that Clark paid James to cover a gambling debt. The money had all of the previously recorded serial numbers.

I am aware that James had alleged that Colt pulled the .22 caliber handgun from his jacket pocket. Colt had nothing to do with the burglary investigation, and the handgun was not recovered during the search of Bradley's home. I have never seen Colt carry a second gun on his person, and I did not see anything to indicate that he was carrying a handgun in his jacket pocket.

After the Nita State Police completed the investigation, Colt and I reviewed this matter with Kathy Cooper, a deputy prosecutor. She declined to file any charges against James for the Bailey controlled buy or the handgun incident involving Colt. She also declined to file a petition to revoke his parole.

The state also sought a bond forfeiture and a bench warrant in Clark's pending criminal case. That warrant still is active, and Clark remains a fugitive. Cooper also declined to file theft charges against Clark for using police money to pay a gambling debt.

I certify that the above is a true and accurate transcript of the deposition of Trace Richards this _____21_____ day of _____December_____ , 2006.

D. J. Sullivan

D. J. Sullivan
Certified Court Reporter

DEPOSITION OF PAT SLATER

My name is Pat Slater, and I am a detective with the Nita State Police. I was a Nita County deputy sheriff for five years before joining the state police in 2003.

If a police officer in the state is involved in a shooting, it is standard practice to have an outside agency conduct the investigation. Nita City has asked the state police to investigate the last several shootings involving their police officers.

On October 3, 2006, I was working the evening shift when I was notified of the shooting of Bart James by Nita City police officer John Colt. I received the call shortly before 5:00 P.M. and arrived at the Nita City police station about thirty minutes later.

The police already had taken possession of the gun, a .22 caliber silver revolver with wooden grips. I placed the gun in a NSP evidence bag for later testing. The gun had five bullets and one spent casing.

I was told that James was taken to Nita General Hospital. I went there to determine his condition. An emergency room nurse told me his injuries were not life-threatening, but that he was scheduled for surgery to remove the bullet from his abdomen. I asked the nurse to make sure that the bullet was placed in a secure location after surgery.

I was given the name of Margaret Brock as a potential witness. I went to her residence when I left the hospital. Brock told me she was in her bedroom around 4:15 P.M. when she saw flashing lights through her front window. When she looked out, she saw an unmarked squad car with another vehicle about 20 feet in front of it.

According to Brock, both drivers were out of their cars when she first saw them. The police officer was not in uniform and was wearing a dark windbreaker. The other man was wearing a gray sweatshirt.

The men were engaged in a heated argument when Brock first saw them, and it appeared that the officer was ordering the other man to get back into his car. After a short period of time, the officer grabbed the man by the right arm and attempted to place him against the car. Brock believed that the officer was attempting to place him under arrest.

The man pulled away the first time, and the officer grabbed him again. The man pulled away a second time. Brock believed that the officer needed assistance, and she dialed 911.

As Brock was identifying herself and starting to explain what was happening, she heard a gunshot. She told the operator a shot had been fired. Brock looked out the window and saw the man lying on the street and the officer holding a gun. Brock reported that the officer had shot someone.

Brock did not see any handgun before the shot was fired. She cannot say who pulled the gun or where it came from. She never left her house or talked to anyone besides the 911 operator.

I called probation officer Chris Panther from my car. He already had been informed of the shooting. Panther told me James had been in compliance with all of the terms of his supervision. He also stated that James was working for his brother, Jack, rehabbing houses.

Panther said James complained to him that Colt had threatened to send him back to prison two times. He said that Colt had made a traffic stop and was upset when James produced a valid driver's license. This incident occurred in June, and Panther told James to let him know if he had any other problems with Colt. James never said anything else to Panther about Colt.

I returned to the hospital to check on James and to see whether the bullet had been recovered. An operating room nurse told me that James had tolerated the surgery well, but that I would not be able to talk to him until the next day. She gave me a .22 caliber bullet, which I placed in a NSP evidence bag.

The nurse also told me James' brother and roommate were waiting for him to come out of the recovery room. She took me to talk to them.

I decided to interview them separately. First, I talked to Bob Carpenter. He told me he and James had gone to the Pit Stop gas station around 4:00 P.M. to collect a gambling debt from Bill Clark. Carpenter told me that Clark paid James $1,000, and James left to play pool at the Sunset Bowling Alley. Carpenter also said James had given him the money for safekeeping, and that Carpenter had placed the money in James' bedroom.

Carpenter also said he gave Clark a ride to the intersection of Broadway and Main on the north side of town. He said he did not know where Clark lived or where he was going.

I then talked to Jack James. He told me he bought houses to rehab and that his brother worked for him. I asked him why his brother was not working the afternoon he was shot, and Jack was evasive. With some prodding, Jack told me that his brother's main source of income was gambling and that he only worked a regular job when he needed some money. Jack also said he did not know Bill Clark or anything about a gambling debt.

On October 4, 2006, I went to the Nita City police station to continue my investigation. I first talked to Lt. William Dennison, who was the shift commander at the time of the shooting. Dennison told me he and the chief were at the mayor's office for a meeting of the public safety commission. Dennison said that the meeting started at 3:00 P.M. and that he did not learn of the shooting until after the meeting.

According to Dennison, the alleged controlled buy violated two department policies. First, a confidential informant must wear a body wire for any controlled buy unless it would create a risk to the confidential informant. The investigating officer is required to get the approval of the shift commander before using a confidential informant who is not wired. Second, an investigating officer must obtain the approval of the shift commander before using more than $500 for a controlled buy. The informant did not wear a body wire, nor did Colt get approval from the shift commander to conduct a controlled buy without a wire.

Dennison told me he had talked to Colt and his partner, Trace Richards, about the violations of department policy. He said that Colt and Richards are excellent police officers and that he understood that they had to move quickly to arrange the controlled buy. Dennison said no disciplinary action would be taken against them because he was not available when the arrangements for the buy were made, and he believed the officers proceeded in good faith.

I next talked to Colt. He agreed to give me a statement without an attorney or a police union representative present. Colt told me he and Richards were responsible for the investigation that led to James' narcotics conviction in 2002.

Colt said he saw James in the courthouse shortly after he was released from prison. Colt admitted he told James that he would be watching him and that he would send James back to jail if he violated his parole.

Colt admitted he stopped James a few weeks later. He knew that James had a suspended driver's license before he went to prison, and Colt assumed he had not obtained a valid license in the short time he was out of jail. When Colt saw the valid license, he gave it back to James and reminded James that he would be watching him.

In August 2006, Richards arrested Mike Bailey on drug charges, and Bailey agreed to cooperate with the police. Bailey told Richards that he had purchased cocaine from James and was willing to make a controlled buy from James. Richards told Colt of this development, and the two of them started working with Bailey to purchase cocaine from James.

According to Colt, in early September 2006, Bailey made several recorded telephone calls to James to arrange the sale. There were some delays because James told Bailey that he only was "working part-time." Bailey finally bought two "8 balls" on September 10, 2006. James also told Bailey not to call him but that he would call Bailey when he had cocaine to sell. Although Bailey saw James a few times after September 10, he was unable to arrange any other buys.

Colt also told me he had arrested Bill Clark for a narcotics violation early in 2006. Clark agreed to cooperate and made several controlled buys before October 3, 2006. None of the buys came from James.

Clark also provided Colt with information concerning a burglary ring in Nita City. Colt knew that Richards was assigned to the case, and he arranged a meeting between Clark and Richards. Based on information provided by Clark, Richards obtained a search warrant and recovered items taken in the burglaries.

When Clark called Colt on October 3 and said he could buy cocaine from James, Colt claimed he had no reason to doubt him. Based on the recorded conversations between Bailey and James, Colt knew that James was selling cocaine on an intermittent basis and that he had to make a buy on James' terms.

Clark called Colt shortly after 3:00 P.M. and told Colt he had received a call from James. Clark also said that he had agreed to meet James at 4:00 P.M. Colt told Clark to come to the police station immediately, and he also paged Richards.

Clark came to the station about fifteen minutes later and told Colt and Richards he had agreed to buy $1,000 worth of cocaine. Colt had tried to talk to Dennison, but he was told that Dennison was at a meeting with the chief and the mayor. Colt and Richards decided to use $1,000 in buy money, even though it required the approval of Dennison.

Nita City has only two body wires: one is a few months old and the other is a few years old. Another narcotics unit had checked out the newer unit. Both Colt and Richards attempted to get the older unit to work, but they could not determine whether there was a mechanical problem or whether it needed new batteries.

By this time it was 3:45 P.M., and they needed to get Clark to the gas station. Colt and Richards decided to proceed with the buy even though they had not informed Dennison that they were using a confidential informant without a body wire.

After conducting the usual search, Colt gave Clark $1,000 in cash and drove to within one block of the Pit Stop. Colt watched Clark walk to the gas station from his surveillance position. Richards was conducting surveillance from across the street in front of Al's Ales, a liquor store in the Shopway strip mall.

About five or ten minutes later, James drove into the gas station and parked his car. Another car parked near James, and a man later identified as Bob Carpenter got out and approached Clark and James.

Colt said he could not see what transpired because the men stood close together. After a few minutes, the three men separated, and James headed back to his car. To Colt's surprise, Clark got into the car with Carpenter.

Colt was in contact with Richards through a police radio. They decided that Colt would follow James, and Richards would follow Clark and Carpenter.

Colt said he was concerned because Clark had left the scene with a target of a drug investigation. Clark had been reliable in the past and had complied with all of Colt's instructions. Colt decided to follow James and stop his vehicle.

James left the gas station on 16th Avenue and turned north on Washington Street. Colt activated the lights on his unmarked car in the 1400 block of Washington Street, and James immediately pulled over and stopped.

Colt was about to report that he had stopped James and request assistance when James got out of his car. Colt did not want James to approach him while he was seated in the squad car, so he quickly got out and ordered James back to his vehicle. James was yelling that Colt was harassing him and refused to return to his car.

Colt approached James and again told him to get back into his car. James was belligerent and repeatedly told Colt that he had no reason to stop him and that Colt was harassing him.

Colt warned James to return to his car or he would be arrested. James refused, and Colt told James he was under arrest. Colt grabbed the right sleeve of James' sweatshirt and told James to lean against the car. James immediately pulled his arm away. However, James did not attempt to push or strike Colt this time.

Colt grabbed James' sleeve a second time in an effort to place him against the car. This time James pulled his arm away and then pushed Colt with both hands. As Colt attempted to grab James a third time, he lifted his arm and pulled away.

As James pulled away the third time, Colt noticed that he lifted the front of his sweatshirt. Colt saw a revolver and immediately reached for it. Colt grabbed the gun and pulled it from the waistband of James' pants. Before Colt could step back, James grabbed the gun with both hands. As they struggled over the gun, it went off.

Colt heard James cry out and knew that James had been shot. James released his grip on the gun and fell to the ground. Colt could see that James was moving and groaning in pain, so he knew that he was not dead.

Colt said that he was stunned and just stood there for a short period of time. He was not sure, but he believed that it may have been a minute or so. As he turned to walk back to his squad car and report the shooting, he heard sirens coming from several directions. He assumed someone had called 911, and he stayed near James.

Patrol officer Lee Butler and Richards arrived on the scene almost simultaneously. Richards told Colt that an ambulance had been dispatched.

The ambulance arrived and the paramedics tended to James and then took him to the hospital. Colt watched as Richards searched the car and said that he did not find any contraband or money. Colt then returned to the station.

I then interviewed Richards. He indicated that he was involved in the original investigation that sent James to jail. Colt told Richards that he had seen James sometime in May 2006. Colt also told Richards, "He won't be out long."

Richards said that he was aware of the traffic stop for allegedly driving without a license. Richards said he and Colt were aware that James had a suspended license before he went to prison.

In August 2006, Richards arrested Mike Bailey for selling cocaine. Bailey agreed to cooperate and told Richards he had purchased cocaine from James since his release from prison. Richards told Colt he had a confidential informant who could buy cocaine from James.

Richards handled the investigation with Bailey as the confidential informant. Several tape recorded telephone calls were made leading to the controlled buy on September 10, 2006.

James had told Bailey that he was only selling cocaine part-time because he knew that Colt was watching him. When Bailey bought the two "8 balls" of cocaine, James told Bailey not to call him and that James would call Bailey if he had any cocaine to sell.

Richards told me Colt arrested Clark in 2006 and that Clark had worked as a confidential informant for Colt for several months prior to the shooting. Richards said that he was investigating a burglary ring in Nita City and that Clark gave Colt some information concerning who was involved and where some other property was located. Richards obtained a search warrant based on this information. The information provided by Clark resulted in the arrest of three individuals and the recovery of stolen property.

Richards received a page from Colt around 3:15 P.M. on October 3, 2006. When he called Colt, Richards was told that Clark had been contacted by James and had agreed to purchase cocaine at 4:00 P.M. Richards returned to the station to meet with Colt and Clark.

Richards confirmed that Dennison was not available as they prepared to make a buy from James. Richards and Colt agreed to use $1,000 in buy money and to send Clark to the site without a body wire because Clark had been reliable in the past and they did not know when they could make a buy from James again.

Richards drove to the Shopway strip mall and got out of his car to watch the proceedings across the street. He saw James drive into the gas station followed by another man later identified as Carpenter. He saw the two men talk to Clark and huddle together as if to hide their hands from public view.

The three men continued to talk as they separated, and James got into his car. Richards saw Clark get into the other car and did not know why that happened. Colt immediately contacted Richards by police radio, and it was agreed that Colt would follow James and Richards would follow the other car.

By the time Richards got back into his car and out of the parking lot, he had lost sight of the vehicle. He drove north on Main Street as fast as he could, but he could not catch up to it. He had proceeded about one mile when he received a dispatch about the shooting in the 1400 block of Washington Street. Richards proceeded directly to the scene and abandoned any attempts to locate Carpenter and Clark.

Richards arrived from the north, and patrol officer Lee Butler arrived from the south at the same time. Richards saw Colt standing next to James and holding a gun, and James lying on the ground. Richards could see that James was moving and in obvious pain.

Richards ran up to Colt and saw that he was visibly upset. Before Richards could say anything, Colt said, "He tried to pull a gun on me." Colt offered the gun to Richards.

Richards asked Colt if he was injured, and Colt said "no." Richards told Colt to put the handgun on the roof of James' car, and he complied. Richards took Colt by the arm to lead him away from the scene. Richards could see that Colt's hands were shaking.

By this time the ambulance had arrived. Paramedic Kim Nomad approached Richards and Colt as the other paramedic went to check James. Colt told Nomad that he was not injured and just needed a few minutes to compose himself. Nomad went to assist James.

Richards then went to participate in the investigation. First he searched the car, but he did not find the buy money, any narcotics, or any paraphernalia. He checked with Nomad and was informed that James' injuries were not life-threatening. Richards asked Nomad to remove all of the items from James' pockets. The search revealed miscellaneous coins, a wallet, and a switchblade that measured eight inches when open. The wallet contained $200, but none of the buy money given to Clark.

After talking to Colt and Richards, I went to the hospital to talk to James. As a precaution, I advised him of his Miranda rights, and he agreed to give a statement.

I asked James a few preliminary questions including his date of birth, address, and occupation. James told me he worked for his brother rehabbing old homes. In response to my question concerning his work schedule for October 3, James said he had worked part of the day and had quit early to play pool at the Sunset Bowling Alley.

James said he stopped to get gas at the Pit Stop before heading north on Washington Street to go to the bowling alley. I asked James whether he saw anyone he knew or talked to anyone in the gas station, and he said "no." I did not confront James with the inconsistency between his story and the statements of his brother and roommate.

James said that he had proceeded a few blocks on Washington Street when he saw flashing lights behind him. He pulled over immediately and saw that he had been stopped by Colt in an unmarked vehicle. James said that he was angry because he had not committed a traffic offense, and he believed Colt was harassing him.

James got out of his car and started to walk back to Colt's vehicle. Colt got out of his squad car quickly and instructed James to return to his car. James said that he stopped walking toward Colt but he refused to get back into his car.

James and Colt continued to yell at each other as Colt approached him. James accused Colt of harassing him, and Colt repeatedly told James to return to his vehicle. In a matter of seconds, Colt was in front of James and threatening to arrest him if he did not get back into his car.

James refused to follow Colt's instructions, and Colt told James that he was under arrest. When James asked why he was being arrested, Colt responded, "You'll find out soon enough." Colt grabbed James by his sweatshirt and attempted to place him against the car. James pulled away and continued to protest his arrest and treatment.

James said that Colt grabbed his sleeve a second time and he pulled away again. James denies striking or pushing Colt during the altercation. When James pulled away the third time, Colt pulled a handgun from his jacket pocket and said, "Now you asked for it."

James knew that Colt was going to shoot him, so he grabbed the gun and tried to push it away from his body. Colt shot him one time before he could point the gun toward the ground.

James said that he felt a sharp pain in his stomach and knew that he had been shot. James remembers some of his treatment by the paramedics and in the emergency room. He says that he was in a lot of pain and blacked out a few times.

James denies that he ever owned a gun or that he had the gun in the waistband of his jeans. James saw Colt's service revolver under his jacket, and he was surprised when Colt produced a second gun during their altercation.

After I completed my interview with James, I delivered the .22 caliber handgun and the bullet recovered during surgery to the NSP crime lab for analysis. Ballistics tests confirmed that the bullet came from the .22 caliber pistol.

The crime lab was unable to recover fingerprints from the gun. This is not unusual, especially since the gun had wooden grips.

Immediately before the shooting, the gun was in either a jacket pocket or a waistband. Pulling the gun from either confined space could obliterate fingerprints. Additionally, Colt and James struggled over the gun. The movement of their hands could have affected any prints that may have been on the handgun.

A review of the police department records showed that the handgun was registered to James Wrigley, 2416 Lilac Avenue, Nita City. The handgun was reported stolen in a burglary on January 29, 2006. Some items taken in the burglary were recovered by Richards based on information provided by Clark. However, no handguns were recovered during the execution of the search warrant.

Clark was arrested on narcotics charges on February 24, 2006. Criminal charges were filed, and Clark was released on an unsecured bond. Because Clark was cooperating with the police, no trial date was set, and Clark remained on bond. When Clark left the area after the alleged buy from James, the state requested a bench warrant for Clark. Neither the police nor the county sheriff has been able to locate Clark.

After completing my investigation, I filed a report with the Nita State Police and provided a copy to the Nita City Police Department.

I certify that the above is a true and accurate transcript of the deposition of Pat Slater this

_____22_____ day of _____December_____, 2006.

D. J. Sullivan

D. J. Sullivan

Certified Court Reporter

DEPOSITION OF JOE SWEENY

My name is Joe Sweeny, and I have known Bart James for five years. We play pool and poker together.

I do not have a criminal record, and I have never sold nor used narcotics. Before James was convicted in 2002, I was aware that he was selling cocaine. I figured that it was his business, and I never said anything to him or to the police.

I have played pool and poker with Bill Clark and Mike Bailey. I heard about their arrests in 2006, but I did not know they were cooperating with the police. I never heard James discussing narcotics transactions with either Clark or Bailey while he was on parole.

James lives with Bob Carpenter, and I have been in their house many times. I never have seen any narcotics, drug paraphernalia, or guns. In all the time that I have known James, I never saw him with a gun.

James was required to get a job as a condition of his parole. He preferred to make a living gambling and only worked for his brother when he was short on cash. James did tell me one time that his brother had written a letter to his parole officer claiming that James was working full-time remodeling houses.

On October 1, 2006, I was playing poker with James, Clark, and two other guys. James won $1,000 from Clark, but Clark did not have enough money to pay James. Clark agreed to pay James within forty-eight hours.

I later learned that James was shot on October 3, 2006, after a meeting with Clark. It appears that Clark conned the police out of $1,000, used it to pay his debt to James, and then left town. I have not seen Clark since October 1, and I do not know where he is. I know that both James and the police would like to see him again.

I certify that the above is a true and accurate transcript of the deposition of Joe Sweeny this

_____22_____ day of _____December_____ , 2006.

D. J. Sullivan

D. J. Sullivan

Certified Court Reporter

REPORT OF THE NITA STATE POLICE

At the request of the Nita City Police Department, the Nita State Police conducted an investigation of the shooting on October 3, 2006, involving Officer John Colt and Bart James. The following facts have been established based on the investigation:

1. On October 3, 2006, Colt was contacted by confidential informant Bill Clark concerning the purchase of cocaine from James.

2. The sale of cocaine allegedly was initiated by James calling Clark, so the telephone call was not recorded.

3. Colt and his partner, Trace Richards, had less than one hour to arrange the controlled buy.

4. Shift Commander William Dennison was not in the police station and was unavailable by telephone.

5. Colt and Richards violated police department procedures by permitting Clark to participate in a controlled buy without a body wire.

6. This violation was not willful because Colt and Richards attempted to obtain a body wire and could not contact Dennison to notify him of the problem.

7. Colt and Richards violated police department procedures when they used more than $500 to purchase narcotics without the approval of Dennison.

8. This violation was not willful because Colt and Richards could not contact Dennison to obtain his approval.

9. The .22 caliber handgun recovered at the scene of the shooting was registered to James Wrigley and reported stolen on January 29, 2006.

10. The burglary of the Wrigley residence was investigated by Richards and solved with the assistance of Clark.

11. On October 3, 2006, Colt had probable cause to believe that James sold cocaine to Clark.

12. Colt was justified in stopping James' vehicle as it left the scene of the alleged controlled buy.

13. When his vehicle was stopped, James got out of his vehicle and refused to return to his vehicle in spite of repeated orders from Colt.

14. Colt had probable cause to arrest James based upon the alleged controlled buy and James' conduct at the scene.

15. James repeatedly resisted arrest when Colt attempted to place him against his vehicle to be searched and handcuffed.

16. James repeatedly lied to the investigating officer and Chris Panther, his parole officer, during the investigation of the shooting. Therefore, the statement of James was not credible.

17. During the struggle to place James under arrest, James attempted to reach for the handgun that was concealed by his sweatshirt.

18. Colt was justified in seizing the handgun.

19. The handgun was discharged inadvertently by Colt during a struggle with James.

20. James was wounded by a single shot from the handgun taken from his waistband.

21. Colt never drew or attempted to draw his service revolver during the incident.

22. Colt did not use excessive force in attempting to arrest James.

23. Clark has disappeared from the area, and there is an outstanding warrant for his arrest.

24. The .22 caliber bullet recovered during surgery came from the handgun recovered at the scene.

25. No fingerprints could be lifted from the handgun.

Discharge Summary

Patient: Bart James

DOB: 1/16/78

Admission 10/3/06

Discharge: 10/6/06

Bart James was brought to Nita Emergency Room on October 3, 2006, at 16:56 hours. His vital signs were stable, and an examination revealed one gunshot wound to the left lower abdomen. There was no exit wound.

The patient was taken to surgery at 17:45 hours, and the bullet was removed and given to the Nita State Police Department.

The patient tolerated the surgery well and was discharged on October 6, 2006. The patient was told to seek additional treatment from his personal physician within seven days.

P. T. Barnes, M.D.
Dictated: 10/7/06

Criminal Record

Name: Bart Andrew James

DOB: 1/16/78

SSN: 987-65-4321

Date of Arrest	Charge	Disposition
8/16/02	Distribution of Cocaine	12/16/02 - Guilty 10 years Nita DOC
5/23/01	Possession of Marijuana	6/26/01 - Guilty $100 fine plus costs
3/17/00	Gambling, Disorderly Conduct	5/21/00 - Guilty Disorderly Conduct, $250 fine plus costs
8/21/98	Minor in Possession of Alcohol, Gambling	10/20/98 - Guilty plea to both counts; 1 year conditional discharge 10/20/99 Case dismissed

Criminal Record

Name: William Harvey Clark

DOB: 3/21/79

SSN: 789-65-1234

Date of Arrest	Charge	Disposition
2/24/06	Possession of Cocaine w/ Intent to Distribute	2/24/06 - Defendant released on $10,000 cash bond. 10/16/06 - Fugitive warrant issued.
11/22/03	Possession of Cocaine w/ Intent to Distribute	2/20/04 - Guilty fine and costs suspended. 1 year incarceration 1 year parole
8/15/00	Possession of Cocaine	1/26/01 - Guilty, fine and costs suspended - 90 days County Jail
7/27/98	Check Deception	9/16/98 - Guilty, $100 plus costs, 1 year probation Restitution $127
3/31/97	Public Intoxication	6/27/97 - Guilty $50 plus costs

Criminal Record

Name: Michael Warren Bailey

DOB: 1/11/80

SSN: 321-45-6789

Date of Arrest	Charge	Disposition
8/21/06	Distribution of Cocaine	11/18/06 - Guilty 6 years Nita DOC
6/10/04	Distribution of Marijuana Possession of Cocaine	1/7/05 - Guilty Possession of Cocaine 2 years probation Distribution of Marijuana dismissed
4/28/03	Public Intoxication	6/1/03 - Guilty $100 plus costs

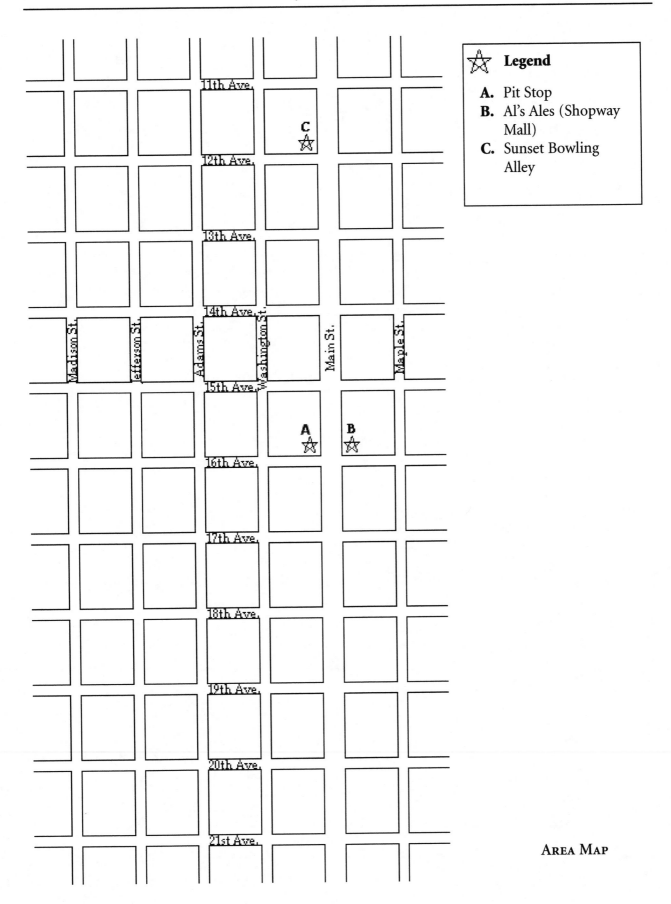

AREA MAP

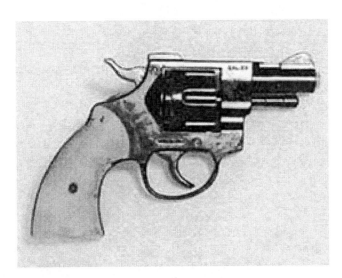

.22 CALIBER HANDGUN

Preliminary Jury Instructions

Duty of Jurors

You have been selected as jurors and have taken an oath to well and truly try this case.

During the trial there will be times when you will be allowed to separate, such as recesses, rest periods, and lunch periods. When you are outside the courtroom, you must not talk about this case among yourselves or with anyone else.

During the trial, do not talk to any of the parties, their lawyers, or any of the witnesses.

If anyone makes any attempt to talk to you concerning this case, you should report the fact to the court immediately.

You should keep an open mind. You should not form or express an opinion or reach any conclusion in this case until you have heard all of the evidence, the arguments of counsel, and the final instructions as to the law.

Issues for Trial

The plaintiff, Bart James, has brought this lawsuit against the defendant, John Colt.

The plaintiff is seeking compensation for the injuries that he received on October 3, 2006. The plaintiff has the burden of proving his claims for damages by a preponderance of the evidence.

The defendant denies the allegations contained in the plaintiff's complaint. The defendant is not required to disprove the claims made by the plaintiff.

Preponderance of the Evidence

When I say that a party has the burden to prove an issue by a preponderance of the evidence, I mean by the greater weight of the evidence. A greater number of witnesses testifying to a fact on one side or a greater quantity of evidence introduced on one side is not necessarily of the greater weight. The evidence given upon any fact that convinces you most strongly of its truthfulness is of the greater weight.

Credibility of Witnesses

You are the sole judges of the credibility or "believability" of each witness and the weight to be given to his testimony. In weighing the testimony of a witness you should consider his relationship to the plaintiff or to the defendant; his interest, if any, in the outcome of the case; his manner of testifying; his opportunity to observe or acquire knowledge concerning the facts about which he testified; his candor, fairness, and intelligence; and the extent to which he had been supported or contradicted by other credible evidence. You may, in short, accept or reject the testimony of any witness in whole or in part.

Concluding Instruction

After I complete these preliminary instructions, the plaintiff and the defendant will have the opportunity to address you in an opening statement. Following the opening statements, first the plaintiff will present evidence and then the defendant will present evidence. After all the evidence has been presented, the parties again will have the opportunity to address you with their final arguments. At the conclusion of this case, I will give you the final instructions to guide your deliberations and to assist you in reaching your verdict.

FINAL JURY INSTRUCTIONS

Plaintiff's Claims

The plaintiff is seeking compensation for his personal injuries based upon the allegation that the defendant used excessive force in making an arrest. The plaintiff also is seeking punitive damages based upon the allegation that the defendant was guilty of willful or wanton misconduct. The defendant has denied these allegations.

Excessive Force

The plaintiff claims that he was subjected to excessive force by the defendant in effecting his arrest. In that regard, you are instructed that every person has the right not to be subjected to unreasonable or excessive force while being arrested by a law enforcement officer, even though such arrest is otherwise made in accordance with due process of law. On the other hand, in making a lawful arrest, an officer has the right to use such force as is necessary under the circumstances to effect the arrest.

Whether the force used in making an arrest was unnecessary, unreasonable, or violent is an issue to be determined by you in the light of all the surrounding circumstances, on the basis of that degree of force a reasonable and prudent officer would have applied in effecting the arrest under the totality of facts and circumstances disclosed in this case. This standard requires that the defendant's liability be determined exclusively upon an examination and weighing of the information that the officer possessed immediately prior to and at the time of the arrest.

Thus, if you find that the defendant used greater force than was reasonably necessary in the circumstances of this case, you must find that the defendant is liable for a violation of the plaintiff's constitutional rights.

The validity of the plaintiff's arrest is irrelevant to the question of whether the defendant used excessive force in effecting the arrest of the plaintiff.

Proximate Cause

Proximate cause is that cause which produces the injury complained of and without which the injury would not have occurred.

Measure of Damages

The plaintiff is required to prove his damages by a preponderance of the evidence. In deciding these damages, you may consider the following:

1. The nature and extent of the injuries.

2. Whether the injuries are temporary or permanent.

3. The physical pain experienced due to the injuries.

4. The reasonable expense of necessary medical care, treatment, and services.

5. Any disfigurement resulting from the injuries.

Your decision must be based on the evidence and not on guess or speculation.

Punitive Damages

If you return a verdict for the plaintiff and you award him compensatory damages, then you may decide to make him a separate and additional award of punitive or exemplary damages against the defendant. You may award punitive damages if you believe that he should be punished for conduct that was motivated by evil motive or malice, or that involves reckless or callous disregard or indifference to the plaintiff's rights.

The plaintiff is not entitled to punitive damages as a matter of right. You must make a judgment about the defendant's conduct. To make such a judgment, it is important to keep in mind that the reason for awarding punitive damages is to punish the defendant for evil motive or malicious conduct against the plaintiff, or callous disregard or indifference for the plaintiff's rights and to deter the defendant and others like the defendant from such conduct in the future. You should consider whether the award of punitive damages will accomplish this dual purpose of punishment and deterrence.

Evil motive or malice means a course of action or inaction on the part of the defendant which, under existing conditions, shows either an utter indifference or a conscious disregard for the rights of others.

Callous or reckless disregard of the consequences is defined as a consciousness of intended or probable effect calculated to unlawfully injure the rights of others.

Deliberations

When you retire to deliberate, select one of your members as the foreman. After you have reached unanimous agreement on your verdict, the foreman must date and sign the verdict form.

CIRCUIT COURT OF DARROW COUNTY

STATE OF NITA

BART JAMES,   )
)
     Plaintiff   )
)
   v.   ) CAUSE NO. 2006 CR 111
)
JOHN COLT,   )
     Defendant   )

Verdict Form

We, the Jury, Find:

_____ In favor of the defendant, John Colt, and against the plaintiff, Bart James.

_____ In favor of the plaintiff, Bart James, and against the defendant, John Colt, and award compensatory damages in the amount of $_____ .

_____ In favor of the plaintiff, Bart James, and against the defendant, John Colt, and award punitive damages in the amount of $_____ .

_____   _____

DATE   FOREMAN